15

RESEARCHING IN A DIGITAL WORLD

How do I teach my students to conduct quality online research?

Erik
PALMER

ASCD   Alexandria, VA USA

Website: www.ascd.org
E-mail: books@ascd.org

www.ascdarias.org

Printed in the United States of America. Cover art © 2015 by ASCD. ASCD publications present a variety of viewpoints. The views expressed or implied in this book should not be interpreted as official positions of the Association. ASCD LEARN TEACH LEAD® and ASCD ARIAS™ are trademarks owned by ASCD and may not be used without permission.

PAPERBACK ISBN: 978-1-4166-2020-4   ASCD product # SF115051
Also available as an e-book (see Books in Print for the ISBNs).

Library of Congress Cataloging-in-Publication Data
Palmer, Erik, 1953-
  Researching in a digital world : how do I teach my students to conduct quality online research? / Erik Palmer.
    pages cm
  Includes bibliographical references.
  ISBN 978-1-4166-2020-4 (pbk.) 1. Internet research--Study and teaching. 2. Report writing--Study and teaching. 3. Report writing--Computer network resources. 4. Research--Study and teaching. 5. Research--Computer network resources. I. Title.
  ZA4228.P35 2015
  001.4'202854678--dc23
                        2014041340

24 23 22 21 20 19 18 17 16 15   1 2 3 4 5 6 7 8 9 10

RESEARCHING IN A DIGITAL WORLD

How do I teach my students to conduct quality online research?

Want to earn a free ASCD Arias e-book?
Your opinion counts! Please take 2–3 minutes to give
us your feedback on this publication. All survey
respondents will be entered into a drawing to
win an ASCD Arias e-book.

Please visit
www.ascd.org/ariasfeedback

Thank you!

The Need for Internet Literacy

Do you send your students to the Internet to do research? I ask teachers this question when I lead workshops, and overwhelmingly, their answer is yes—even in the primary grades. Then I ask if they teach any specific lessons to *prepare* students for researching in an online environment. Equally overwhelmingly, their answer is no. Because our students are digital natives, right? Even the youngest of them seems able to intuit how to manipulate all kinds of digital devices, how to create and upload content, and how to find entertaining things online. This leads us to assume they are Internet competent and completely web savvy. But do they really understand how to find the best of places for research and how to analyze all the sites their device dexterity helps them find? The answer is no.

Here is something else I've learned from my workshops: Teachers absolutely believe that teaching Internet literacy is necessary. Yet it isn't happening—and not because of the time constraints, although that is certainly a factor. The main issue is that many of us don't have a great deal of Internet literacy ourselves. The intricacies and operation of Wikipedia, domain name suffixes, search engines, browsers, how to find who is publishing particular site content, how Google decides what to list first on a search page, how to use punctuation to get better search results—for many of us, these remain mysteries.

Student Struggles with Online Research

I happened to be in Oregon recently. As you may know, that part of the country is the home of the endangered Pacific Northwest tree octopus (*Octopus paxarbolis)*, the cephalopod that is born in the ocean but comes ashore to live in the forests along the Oregon coast. I wrote about the animal and the website devoted to it (http://zapatopi.net/treeoctopus/) in my book *Teaching the Core Skills of Listening & Speaking* (Palmer, 2014). I didn't see any tree octopi on any of my walks, but I didn't expect to—unlike many of the students I've taught, who visited the website and had trouble recognizing it as an elaborate hoax. The trip reminded me of the kinds of struggles students have with online research:

- Uncertainty about what words to put into the browser's search box
- Overreliance—often *exclusive* reliance—on Google
- Difficulty figuring out which of the 34,219,300 search results returned is the best place to start
- Never looking beyond the first page of results
- Inability to assess the purpose of a site
- Never checking or considering the authority of the site's authors
- Not knowing how to evaluate a site's credibility
- Copying information and images without understanding plagiarism or copyright

These and other issues make clear that we have some work to do to prepare our students before we send them online. Without that preparation, projects that could engage students in independent learning and critical thinking end up wasting learning time, yielding bad information, and creating both bad habits and faulty understanding.

Much of what I will share in this book was learned the hard way. For years, I had my students do a research project I called "Planetary Problem Solving"—a project easily adaptable to all grade levels and a variety of subject areas. The set-up was simple: Choose a current global problem (e.g., acid rain, overpopulation, world hunger, heart disease), research it, and report out, citing at least three online references. What I didn't do was provide any instruction to build my students' Internet literacy. Problems followed.

I have structured this book in a way that I hope is useful. We will proceed through the process of researching online. In each section, I will give some background knowledge to share with students and then use a Planetary Problem Solving example—childhood obesity—to illustrate how this insight might be applied. In the end, I hope you will walk away with a practical approach for preparing your students to conduct truly effective online research.

The Challenge for Teachers

Let's be honest: the Internet was not designed with students in mind—and certainly not elementary students. I once watched a 2nd grade teacher hand each student a Chromebook, assign them a country to report about, and direct them to www.safesearchkids.com. After that, she left them to their own devices. Students inputted "Brazil" or "Italy" and got flooded with results—all kinds of sites, both credible and dubious. The kids who weren't distracted by ads and pop-ups dutifully copied information into their notebooks, even words and information they didn't understand.

The digital natives in our classroom still need our guidance in the form of information that will help them be savvier and more efficient researchers. They need our support in the form of practical strategies that they can use to think more critically about the "facts" they find online. Adapt the ideas in this publication for your grade level. Modify its action items as needed. And always be vigilant as your students search, especially if they are very young.

Before Students Go Online

Our students have never known a world without the Internet, but that doesn't mean that they couldn't benefit from a little tutorial about some of the basics of its operation. Let's start there.

Logistics and Key Terms

What is happening when we "go online"? It is useful for students (and adults) to understand some key terms and logistics.

The Internet is not a place. Nor is it an all-knowing, all-wise source of knowledge. It is a vast network of interconnected computers. Students commonly say, "I found it on the Internet," yet the information we find when we research is not "on the Internet"; it's on some computer tied in to that network. This is important knowledge to share with students to begin creating a healthy skepticism. We can't be sure of the validity of the information found on the computers tied into the network. The Internet itself is not a resource; it's what allows us to access resources.

Back in the 1990s, when the Internet was taking off, it was common to talk about it as "the World Wide Web." The terminology seems quaint now, and your students may not even recognize the "www." at the beginning of Internet addresses as its abbreviation. But it really is helpful to think of the Internet as a worldwide web—a collection of documents and other resources that have been formatted with Internet protocols that allow them to be accessed. The most common of these protocols is the Hyper Text Transfer Protocol, which gives us the "http:" in Internet addresses. Your computer is part of the Internet because your router, cable, and wires link you to the network; the files on your personal computer (lesson plans and family photos, among others) are not part of the Internet because they are not formatted in a web-searchable way.

A browser gives you access to the Internet. Web browsers are computer programs that access files linked to the web and display them on your computer. "Plug-ins" built into the software allow you to see documents, videos, games, and images, and to hear audio from files and other computer users. It is common in schools for students to get a message similar to "File cannot be displayed. Plug-in required." This means that the browser does not have the software needed to display the media.

There are lots of browsers available. Microsoft computers come with Internet Explorer installed; Apple computers come with Safari. There are also Firefox, Google Chrome, Bing, Opera, Torch, SeaMonkey, and many, many more. Each has its fans. A browser is generally judged by how fast it loads; how often it crashes; how easily it allows a user to create and organize bookmarks and tabs; whether it includes features like auto-fill, password memorization, and customizable pages; and so on. Browsers all have a URL line, the place where we input the Uniform Resource Locator (URL)—the web address. If we know the address of a site, we can simply input it and go straight to the site. Similarly, sometimes teachers have great sites they want students to visit, and they can just provide the links. That's easy. It is also not the topic of this book. The real fun begins when we don't give students the answer and ask them to go looking.

Action Item: Internet Terminology 101. Review with students the definitions of *Internet, web, browser,* and *URL*. As appropriate for your grade level, ask questions to ensure that they understand the key terms in Internet searching. Create or have students create a visual flowchart of the process of searching. For example, show the process "a URL tells the browser what you're looking for, and the browser searches the web. The web is searchable because of the Internet." Adapt the language as necessary for your grade level.

Crafting Questions to Guide Research

A 6th grade health teacher wants her students to find out about the harmful effects of cigarette smoking. Kim volunteers to find information online and report back to the class. He enters "cigarette smoking" in the search box at www.google.com. He returns to class with his facts:

- Eighteen percent of high school boys smoke cigars.
- In 1964, 42 percent of adults smoked cigarettes.
- It is common for people gain 5 to 10 pounds when they quit smoking.

This *is* information related to smoking, but none of it fulfills the purpose of the assignment: to explain the harmful effects of smoking cigarettes. What went wrong?

Research is about finding answers. This seems like an obvious statement to make, but it carries an important truth that's easy to forget: finding answers assumes you have questions. Students doing research typically say things such as, "I am looking up Brown v. Board of Education" or "I am researching Albert Einstein," or, in Kim's case, "I am finding out about cigarette smoking."

We can trace Kim's research problem to the way he phrased his search. Without good guiding questions, students like Kim find and write down all kinds of random and trivial facts, winding up with an unfocused collection of information. Effective research, then, begins with meaningful questions. Having students brainstorm search questions and winnow them down into a tight list is a way to promote focused, efficient online research and lead students to an understanding of big ideas.

Action Item: What's the Question? In the primary grades (K–2), it's best to think of online searches as scavenger hunts designed to familiarize students with what it means to use the Internet to find information. Give them a form with key search questions related to the topic they are studying. For example, if everyone has chosen an animal to research, you might provide this set of questions:

1. How tall is this animal?
2. How much does this animal weigh when it is an adult?
3. Where does this animal live?
4. What does this animal eat?

In grades 3 and above, try putting students in groups of three or four to brainstorm guiding questions. Challenge them to generate as many Who, What, When, Where, Why, and How questions as they can for each topic. A 9th grader investigating childhood obesity might collaborate with classmates to generate questions such as these:

1. What makes kids obese?
2. What health problems are caused by obesity?
3. What social problems do obese kids have?
4. What is the definition of obese?
5. What is the difference between obese and overweight?
6. What are some ways children can lose weight?
7. What percent of kids are obese now?
8. What percent of adults are obese?

9. What country has the most obese children?

10. How likely is it that obese kids will grow up to be obese adults?

Ask students to give each question a ranking: "I absolutely have to find this out," "I'd like to find this out," or "I could skip this." The questions that interest them most and seem most important are those they should use to begin their research. Step in as needed to review the students' questions and keep them moving toward an essential understanding of the topic.

Formatting Search Questions

Typically, students can enter the questions they generate (or you provide) directly into the search box of most search engines. This approach often produces better results than entering one or two key words. But there are other ways to frame a question for Internet searching—ways that will not only generate a more focused collection of relevant results but also challenge students to think creatively and critically as they search.

Boolean searches. A good librarian will tell students to refine searches with Boolean search terms. George Boole was a 19th-century mathematician credited with developing a new area of algebra. There were three key operations in his system: AND, OR, and NOT. Often, adding these operations to search questions can produce more efficient search results.

- *Add AND:* Typing AND (or &) between key words will yield only results where both terms are present. If we think in terms of a Venn diagram, *AND* returns results that fall in the intersection of the circles—not resources linked to any of the key words but resources linked to both. Let's say I already have information about how the number of obese children in the United States has changed over the last few years. Entering *childhood obesity AND health risks* into my search engine will limit the results to resources that discuss the health risks correlated with childhood obesity; entering *childhood obesity AND school problems* will target information about how schools are affected by the problem.

- *Add OR:* Typing OR (or /) between key words will return results that include either or both key words. It's a good choice when researchers aren't sure what key words will pull up the information they're looking for. Perhaps I'm curious how obesity affects high school students. Entering *teen OR teenage OR adolescent AND obesity* will cast a wider net and bring more results.

- *Add NOT:* With some search engines, inserting *NOT* (or –) between key words will limit the search results. This is especially useful if the search terms entered have multiple meanings. Entering *oxygen* will take you to a TV network, an element in the periodic table, a Google font, an XML editor, and more. Knowing you don't need all possible uses of the word, you can put NOT before the usages you don't want. NOT can also be used to narrow a search. If I have all the numbers I need about obesity in the United States, I can enter *childhood obesity NOT United States* to find data about other countries only.

Search shortcuts. You have probably had the experience of entering multiple words in a search box and getting results that contain all those words but have other words in between. Perhaps you got results with slightly different spellings. For example, here's what I got when I searched my name, Erik Palmer:

Erik Palmer-Brown
Karl **Erik Palmer**
Eric Palmer
Erik Christensen a member of the **Palmer** Arkansas Rotary Club

These off-topic dead ends could've been avoided with the simple use of quotation marks. Searching "Erik Palmer" notifies the spiders (see p. 15) that they should only look for the complete phrase exactly as I typed it. When I entered *childhood obesity and health* into my search bar, it returned 8,400,000 results. By contrast, entering *"childhood obesity and health"* returned only results with that complete phrase together—still a daunting 286,000 results, but a little bit more manageable.

There are lots of useful shortcuts like this to pass on to students. It's likely that the search engine you use in your classroom has a cheat sheet available. Google's shortcuts, for instance, are offered and explained at https://support.google.com/websearch/answer/136861. Whatever engine you use, type "[search engine name] *shortcuts*" into your search bar to find a similar list.

Here are some more search shortcuts I recommend:

- *Add the prefix SITE: to focus on particular domain types.* If students are seeking government data or, say, looking to avoid information on .com sites (more about that on p. 27), typing *site:* and then the desired domain type before the search terms will limit the search to those kinds of sites. As an education author, I often limit my searches to .edu sites (*site:.edu*). *Childhood obesity* returned 16,000,000 hits with every possible domain suffix, but *site:.org childhood obesity* eliminated all sites except for those with a .org suffix and returned a more modest 400,000 results.

- *Add the prefixes RELATED: and LINK: to continue down a promising path.* One good source can lead to another. When students find a page that contains particularly useful or relevant material, they can find similar sites by typing *related:* before the site address. For example, *related:www.healthychildren.org* will look for pages with content similar to what's available at www.healthychildren.org. Scholarly sites will likely have other websites that link to them or that use them as a bibliographic resource. Students can find out if others have found a site useful by entering *link:* into the search box before the site's URL. Close to 22 million sites link to an article on childhood obesity that I found at the website of the Centers for Disease

Control and Prevention, suggesting that quite a few folks think the article is worth a look.

- *Add the prefix FILETYPE: to find information in specific formats.* Perhaps students would like to find information in a certain file type—a PowerPoint (.ppt) presentation, maybe? They can enter *filetype: ppt.* Entering *childhood obesity filetype: ppt* into my search bar found the 11,000 PowerPoint presentations on this topic that are available on the web.

There are plenty of other shortcuts to explore and recommend; I've listed only the ones I've found most useful. The key is to let students know that finding better answers to their questions can be a matter of finding better ways to frame their searches.

Action Item: Strategic Questioning. When students have generated a list of search questions, put them in groups to have them translate these questions into the most strategic search format. For example "What health problems are correlated with obesity?" might translate to *obesity AND health problems.* "What is the definition of obese?" would be *definition: obese.* Groups can discuss where quotation marks ought to be used and where it might be useful to look for certain types of files. If the objective is to find information on the percentage of obese children, does it make sense to look for PowerPoint files, which often contain lots of graphs and visuals? Provide suggestions as needed to help students see possibilities.

Going Online to Seek Answers

When students have this background about the searching process, when they have important guiding questions, and when they have a few ideas about how to speak the search language, they are ready to research. It's time to go online.

Pew Research Center (2012) interviewed middle and high school teachers to find out about student research habits. One query asked what tools students use. Here are some of the results:

- 94 percent use Google or some other search engine.
- 75 percent use Wikipedia or other online encyclopedia.
- 52 percent use YouTube or other social media.
- 17 percent use databases (e.g., EBSCO, JSTOR).
- 16 percent use a research librarian at their school or public library.
- 10 percent use student-oriented search engines (e.g., SweetSearch). (p. 4)

Should the percentages be different? I'll argue yes, they should. I'll share some information in this section that I hope will persuade you (and your students) to value these tools differently.

Search Engines

Search engines are programs designed to help us find the web pages that are related to our search terms. These programs send "spiders" out to scan the web for matches and return what is often a massive index of websites.

When you think about search engines, the first that comes to mind is probably Google, which has become to search engines what Kleenex is to facial tissues and Xerox is to photocopiers. In August 2014, it was estimated that Google got 1,100,000,000 unique monthly visitors, about three times as many visits as the nearest competitor (eBizMBA, 2014). But in addition to Google and fellow all-purpose search engines like Bing, Yahoo!, and Ask, there is a whole world of specialized search engines on the web. Ever look up a medical problem at WebMD? Ever look for a video on YouTube? Check real estate prices on Zillow? Get directions from MapQuest? Those are all examples of search engines with a focus. You can get an idea of many of these possibilities by looking at the list of search engines and categories at www.thesearchenginelist.com.

The opposite end of the spectrum exists, too. In addition to narrowly focused search engines, there are metasearch engines with a very broad reach. Think of the various travel websites we use to help us find flights, hotels, and rental cars. I can check for flights, for example, at United's website, Frontier's website, Southwest's website, American's website, and Expedia's website, among others. Or I can check all of them at once using the metasearch engine called Kayak. Metasearch engines don't send spiders through the web. Instead, they send your query to the search engines that send spiders, and then they compile all of those results, filtering out duplicates. Older students should consider using

Dogpile, an all-purpose metasearch engine (www.dogpile.com). As with Google, the first few results are ads, but the "Web Results" for my "childhood obesity" prompt yielded a lot of high-quality sites.

Specialized search engines for students. We know that the web contains much that is inappropriate for children, and schools have taken various steps to protect students and send them to "safe sites," including installing various kinds of filters that block "adult" content. Another option, though, is to restrict students to special search engines made for them.

All of the search engines listed below were created with the goal of protecting children from inappropriate material, but many have the added advantage of being specially designed to make school-appropriate searching easier. Be aware, however, that "Safe Search" means adult content has been eliminated, but adult vocabulary has not. Look at each of these and try a few searches about various topics that come up in your grade. Find the ones that return grade-appropriate reading levels. Teachers of grades K–3 will love KidRex; AP History teachers will love Google Scholar.

- Kidsclick! (www.kidsclick.org)—designed by librarians, it allows students to search by key words, categories (Biography, Machines, Health), media (Pictures, Sound), and even Dewey decimal numbers.
- KidzSearch (www.kidzsearch.com)—one of the most popular, but it is cluttered by the same ads found in a regular Google search.

- KidRex (www.kidrex.org)—high-quality sources dominate the main results page; ad free.
- SweetSearch (www.sweetsearch.com) and the related site for younger students, SweetSearch4me (http://4me.sweetsearch.com)—the results are displayed with key callouts from the resource, giving students a glimpse of what will be found in the entire article and a quick way to judge if the resource will meet their needs. SweetSearch2day (http://2day. sweetsearch.com) offers a daily assortment of sites that can be used for quick Internet lessons, discussion starters, "This day in history" information, and more.
- GoGooligans (www.gogooligans.com)—designed for younger students, this search engine's returned results include Google ads but are also grouped into potentially helpful categories (e.g., Facts, Economy, History, Research). Entering *childhood obesity* generates a list of resources, of course, but clicking on one of the category tabs generates specific lists (e.g., articles containing statistics about obesity, articles explaining the costs of obesity, articles about obesity over time, research papers about obesity).
- Google Scholar (http://scholar.google.com)—results are retrieved from research articles, works produced by academic publishers, journals of professional organizations, college and university websites, and other "scholarly" sources.

- ipl2 (www.ipl.org)—results are returned from a curated collection of resources assembled by a group of volunteer information science professionals and librarians. Searches yield fewer sources, but they are thoroughly vetted. Searching "childhood obesity" gave me 148 results when I selected the "Search all of ipl2" option. Switching to the "For Teens" search option yielded one result of marginal usefulness, and switching to "For Kids" yielded one result of reasonable usefulness.

Action Item: Un-Googling. At the start of a project, challenge students to use any search engine other than plain old Google.

Action Item: Engine Exploration. Model a search for students in which you enter the same key words into different search engines. Ask students what they notice. Does one search engine appear more "kid friendly" than the others? More visually appealing? Do ads distract? Do they all return the same number of results? Why might a Google search of "childhood obesity" yield more than 20 million results, a KidRex search yield less than 8 million, and a Google Scholar search only 800,000? Are the types of results different (one has more .coms; one has more images displayed, etc.)? Are results easier to understand on one site compared to others?

Action Item: "Advanced" Searching. With upper elementary students and above, look for an "Advanced Search" tab or a "Search Tools" tab on the search page. Point out to students that these functions allow them to refine their searches by, for example, limiting results to recent information or information at a certain reading level. Only 24 percent of my Google search results about childhood obesity were at a "Basic" reading level, so an elementary teacher who showed her students how to select that level would drastically improve the efficiency of their searches.

Websites

Now, with our search questions entered, let's look more closely at exactly what the spiders have found for us. When I searched for "childhood obesity," Google Scholar found 800,000 results. What *are* those results? They are pages found on websites. Google Scholar clearly lists the name of the website that houses each result: "from nih.gov," "from allhealth.org," and so on. Not all search engines identify websites this clearly, but generally, the names are discoverable. My KidRex search of our topic found this result:

kidshealth.org/parent/general/body/overweight_**obesity**.html

Perhaps it is clear to you what the website is, but will all of your students be able to see it? How about this one?

thecolbertreport.cc.com/videos/7vvoyf/michelle-obama-vs--**child-obesity**

I will talk about evaluating websites a little later on, but that discussion will not make sense to students unless they understand this key point: search engines find resources housed on a website, and websites are not equally reliable in terms of factual information appropriate for academic research. Kidshealth.org is qualitatively different from the website of *The Colbert Report.*

Library Databases

Does anyone else remember using the *Readers' Guide to Periodical Literature*? It was an index of hundreds of magazines. You could open the book to the page containing your topic and find out that *Time* had an article about it in December 2001, *Forbes* had one in 2002, and so on. Then you'd talk to the librarian, who would disappear into a back room and come out with a box of old magazines labeled "Time, Oct 2001 to Jan 2002." If all went well, you'd find the issue you needed.

Think of a library database along those lines—it's an index of published works. The essential point for researchers is the word *published.* That means authors are likely to be experts in their field, and editors have checked facts. In a library database, students will find a collection of articles from journals, magazines, newspapers, books, reference materials (encyclopedias, dictionaries, atlases), and more. Some databases are general and broad-ranging in nature, and others are quite specific. For example, my local library, Aurora Public Library, subscribes to databases from EBSCO Information Services. These include Academic Search Premier, a general database including 4,600 journals, as well as Small Engine Repair Reference Center, a quite specific database indeed.

We can add other search engine possibilities here. The Aurora Public Library has Searchasaurus, Kidsearch, and Student Research Center. These are search engines that can find information within all of the databases available. Designed for students of different ages, all of them will produce results restricted to published articles, of course. My library also has Primary Search (accessing articles from 70 different magazines for elementary students); Middle Search Plus (accessing articles from 140 magazines for middle school students, plus biographies, plus primary source documents); and Points of View (accessing coverage of current events under debate).

From a researcher's perspective, there are enormous advantages to using library databases. So what's the catch? Cost and access. These databases are not free, and libraries pay significant fees to be able to offer these research options. Although many public libraries do allow their patrons to access databases remotely, through online interfaces, it is necessary to be a registered library card holder. Not all students will be.

Action Item: Web vs. Database. Get students thinking about the key features of websites and library databases and how they differ. You might, for example, create and discuss a table like the one shown in Figure 1, or solicit student input to create this comparison.

FIGURE 1: **Websites Versus Library Databases as Information Sources**

Websites	Library Databases
There are ads	There are no ads
Materials can written by anyone	Materials are more likely to be written by experts
Information may not be verified	Information has been checked
There is no guarantee info has been updated	Sources are constantly updated
Can feature any kind of writing	Features only writing that has been published elsewhere
Material has various intended purposes (to entertain, to persuade, to sell)	Purpose is to provide information
Access is free	Access is limited to library members, and those who pay significant subscription fees
Articles may cost money	Once accessed, full article text is free
It may or may not be clear who the author is	The author is clearly named

Action Item: Public Library Field Trip. Direct students to the closest public library, and task them with asking a librarian to explain the databases the library offers. Ask the students to make a list of databases that seem especially useful for them. Encourage students to use these databases in their research.

Action Item: School Library Field Trip. I taught in the Cherry Creek School District for many years. This district has a number of databases available for all of its students. One is Pebble Go, a group of databases for "emergent readers" (www.pebblego.com). It is excellent. Chances are your district has similar offerings. Check to see if your school or district subscribes to some databases, and include them on the list of resources students must use.

Journal Databases

Music therapists do not make up a huge segment of the workforce. Even so, they have their own journal, the *Journal of Music Therapy*. Take a moment to investigate, and you'll discover that nearly every profession and interest group has a specific periodical devoted to its interests. Microbiology? Check. Game theory? Check. Microwave science? Check. Ecology, consumer marketing, nursing ethics? Check, check, and check. I entered "journal of childhood obesity" in a search engine. Surprise! There is a journal for childhood obesity: *Childhood Obesity*. It's published bimonthly.

Obviously, a scholarly journal written *by* people in the field *for* people in the field would be a useful place to find information. A few cautions, though. First, journals are likely to be useful for upper-grade students only. They are not written for children. Second, journal articles are likely to have a fee attached. Often, you can find an abstract online, but the full text must be purchased. Having access to *Childhood Obesity*'s August 2014 issue for 24 hours will cost you $51. (If your library subscribes to the journal, the full text will be available to you.) Finally, having the word "journal" in the title is not a guarantee of scholarly content. Realizing that being published in a journal conveys some credibility, some companies produce pay-for-inclusion journals. The *New York Times* has written about "the proliferation of online journals that will print seemingly anything for a fee. They warn that nonexperts doing online research will have trouble distinguishing credible research from junk" (Kolata, 2013).

Wikipedia

If your students are doing online research, they will find a Wikipedia article. That is almost certain. Like all wiki files, the articles on Wikipedia are files that can be edited by anyone, and the site is quite clear about this:

> Welcome to Wikipedia, the free encyclopedia that *anyone can edit.* 4,579,763 articles in English. (Wikipedia, 2014c, emphasis added)

It is important for students recognize Wikipedia for what it is: a collective resource generated by users, and perhaps a good place to start research and gain a general introduction to a topic but not definitive or even necessarily reliable on its own.

All articles on Wikipedia have tabs on the upper right of the page. There is the default "Read" tab that the site opens, usually an "Edit" tab, and a "View history" tab. Clicking on the Edit tab opens a page that lets you alter the article much the same way as you change a Word document on your computer. Clicking on the View history tab will show how often and how recently the article has been edited.

If you open the "Childhood Obesity" article on Wikipedia (2014a), you will notice that the Edit tab has been replaced by a "View source" tab. Wikipedia makes this swap for subjects that are likelier to be targets for vandalism. Only "registered users" can edit such pages, but inclusion on the "approved for editing" list does imply those users have subject expertise; it simply means they have not demonstrated an intent to mislead.

Action Item: Wikipedia Archeology. Show students the history of a Wikipedia article. Discuss why the article may have been changed. Has new information about the subject become available? For high school students, find the "Compare selected revisions" tab at the bottom of the history page. Select a random revision and let students see how the process has worked.

Evaluating Online Resources

If students have done their work well, seeking answers will have led them to lots of places that contain information they need. But how can they sift through all of those possibilities? Let's focus on some ways to do that.

When I was in school, research meant going to the *World Book Encyclopedia.* I never gave a second thought to evaluating its credibility. It seems we have come a long way from those simple days. Today, it is critical to instill in students a healthy cynicism, to give them a few tools for analyzing the sources of information they find, and to guide them toward valuable information from credible resources.

According to the Pew Research survey mentioned earlier, "Seventy-six percent of teachers surveyed 'strongly agree' with the assertion that Internet search engines have conditioned students to expect to be able to find information quickly and easily . . . the amount of information available online today is overwhelming to most students (83% [agree]) . . . a majority . . . (60%) agree with the assertion that today's technologies make it harder for students to find credible sources of information" (2012, p. 3). As one of the surveyed teachers lamented, students "cut and paste without reading or evaluating" (p. 24). Let me share some tips, then, for empowering students to separate the signal from the noise.

Website Evaluation

Search engines do not list resources according to scholarly value. Indeed, when we use Google to search "childhood obesity," the first listings are ads—sites that paid for their position. Listings after those are based on algorithms that factor in presence of key words, frequency of key words, links to and from the site, and past search history, among other things.

Google admits that "Our automated systems analyze your content (including emails) to provide you personally relevant product features, such as customized search results, tailored advertising, and spam and malware detection. This analysis occurs as the content is sent, received, and when it is stored" (Google, 2014, para. 16).

Action Item: The Winner Isn't in First Place. With students in the upper grades, go over the topic of customized search results, stressing the idea that the top results on the page are not necessarily the "best" results but rather the results that the search engine believes you will like. Try an experiment: Give half the class a short set of *Huffington Post* links to access and the other half, a short set of *Fox News* links. Take one computer from each group, open up the same search engine, search on the same term, and project the results onto your screen or whiteboard. Compare the results that rise to the top.

So, how can students figure out if a website is a good source of information? There is no one test that determines value. We can't say, "All .com sites are bad" or "All pages with more ads than information are worthless." We have to give students a few ways to assess website value so that they can decide whether, on balance, the site is worthy of their time and the information is worthy of being recorded.

Examine domain type. What type of domain suffix is being used? There is a difference between .com and .edu, and students need to know that difference. Let me repeat some of what I wrote in *Teaching the Core Skills of Listening & Speaking,* adding a "Caveat Emptor" credibility rating: 4 = Be very suspicious; 3 = Be suspicious; 2 = Be slightly suspicious; 1 = Everything is the guaranteed truth.

- .com is the most commonly used extension and the one that comes to mind for most people. The "com" stands for commercial, which is the signal that . . . [a] student should expect to see something for sale . . . the information they find may be reliable, but they should watch out for the pitch. *Rating: 4.*

- .net is an abbreviation for network; it was originally for businesses that provided the services the web depends upon (Internet service providers and web hosting companies). Now anyone can buy a .net domain name. *Rating: 4*

- .org is an abbreviation for organization. Although it is still primarily used by groups, associations, and organizations, it too is now an extension that can be purchased by anyone. Tell students that .org sites may have more expertise behind them than .com sites . . . they're more likely to find reliable information from www.cancer.org, the website of the American Cancer Society, than from a .com . . . [but] it does not mean [a .org] is bias free.

The National Rifle Association, www.nra.org, for example, has a message to convey. *Rating: 3*

• .gov is an abbreviation for government, and it is truly is restricted to entities of the federal, state, and local governments. *Rating: 2*

• .edu is an abbreviation for education . . . (colleges, universities, and community colleges) . . . the quality of information vetted through an educational website has a higher probability of reliability than something on a .com, for instance. *Rating: 2.* (Palmer, 2014, p. 73)

Notice I didn't give any domain a 1 rating. While .gov sites have a better overall credibility, in my opinion, than .coms, many .gov sites are biased in favor of the party currently in power. Although .edu sites may be written and peer-reviewed by professors, those professors may have biases, too. Also notice that I did not even mention the new gimmicks in domain names (.guru, .expert, .guide, .ninja, etc.). Stay away from these.

Examine site appearance. Sometimes a quick glance can reveal a lot. Does it say "professional and scholarly"? Or does it say "dodgy and cheap"? I don't want to disparage all nonprofessional sites, but I do want to encourage more critical thinking in student researchers. Here's a process I recommend:

1. Get a quick sense of the amount of information shown. At first glance, does there seem to be a lot of information?

What is the ratio of advertisements to information? Are potentially valuable images and graphics immediately noticeable, or are pop-ups competing for your attention?

2. Explore a few links. If there are links to other pages or websites, click on some. Do they dead-end in "404 Page Not Found"? Do they lead to useful information on other sites? Do they lead to commercial sites or non-related pages?

3. Look for dates. Has the site been updated recently? If all the posts are old, it's an indication that the site creator has given up on the site.

Consider site purpose. If students have chosen their search engine wisely and formatted their questions well, the results returned should be limited to informational sites. There is no guarantee of that, however, so we have to ask students to spend a minute or two questioning the purpose of the site:

- Is it to sell them products?
- Is it to persuade them to do or believe something?
- Is it to divert or entertain them?
- Is it to inform them?

Action Item: Dueling Websites. Ask students to compare how two or three different websites address the same topic. For childhood obesity, you might look at an article published by a government entity, like the Centers for Disease Control; an article from a mainstream magazine website (e.g., *Time* or *U.S. News*); and a commercial site's announcement of a new app designed to help kids lose weight through physical activity. With young students, direct the discussion: Did they notice all of the ads on the pages? Did they notice blue words in the middle of some sentences? Are those words helpful? Do they understand all the words on the page? How can we tell who made this website? Do they know about *U.S. News*—a magazine that is sold at bookstores? Is a magazine's website a good place to look for information? Allow older students to direct the discussion themselves, but ask them to decide, based on their first impressions of the search results returned, which site would be the best choice for information for a research paper. Call for a vote, and have students explain why they voted the way they did.

Examine site ownership. Remember that a search engine will return pages housed at specific website. But who is responsible for that information, that page, that site? Most often, site ownership information can be found via links labeled "Home," "About Us," "About," "FAQ," or something similar, placed on a tab at the top of the page, but it may be necessary to hunt for this information via links labeled "Contact Us," "Advertise," or "Terms of Service."

With long web addresses, show students how to truncate—to cut off the URL after the domain name suffix. For example, cutting everything after the .org in the search result *kidshealth.org/parent/general/body/overweight_***obesity**. *html* will take us more quickly to the information we want about the KidsHealth site. Yes, this can be a hassle, but stress to students that it is the first step in some essential detective work.

When I used SweetSearch, I found an article, "Obesity in Children," at this address: http://www.nlm.nih.gov/medlineplus/obesityinchildren.html. Clearly visible at the top of the article is a link labeled "About MedlinePlus," the website hosting the article. One click revealed that "MedlinePlus is the National Institutes of Health's Web site" (Medline Plus, 2013). And what is the National Institutes of Health (NIH)? Another clearly marked link takes you to the explanation that NIH is the part of the U.S. Department of Health and Human Services devoted to medical research.

Teach students to spend two, or three, or five minutes looking into site credentials and authorship. Yes, this is time they could be spending recording information on notecards, but without spending that time, they won't really know if they *should* be copying information from the site.

Action Item: Hunting for Nonsense. Take younger students to visit the website Save the Rennets (http://savetherennets.com). The home page explains the horrible things being done to these adorable creatures. Then find the About Us link at the bottom of the home page. It will be immediately obvious why it is important to find this tab: "We have just made most of this up."

Action Item: Who Owns This? As your class gears up for online research, select a student to do a search of her topic as the rest of the class looks on. When she finds a result that she thinks may be useful, ask her to think aloud about the process of looking for ownership. Can she easily find out who is behind this website? If she can, does she think that the people or organization responsible are likely to be knowledgeable about the topic? Should she begin taking notes for her report?

Consider authority. *Who wrote this, and why should I believe this writer?* These are key questions for researchers to ask about every text resource they consult. When students access journal articles, authorship and credentials are immediately available; with articles on websites, the issue of authority isn't so easily settled.

Sometimes the site sponsor has authority—NIH, for example, or the Mayo Clinic—but not all students will recognize this legitimacy. Encourage your students to ask questions: Does the Mayo Clinic have something to do with mayonnaise? Is the *New York Daily News* a respectable news source? How can they find out? If the site sponsor doesn't have obvious authority, it is crucial to find an author's name. Is the author someone whose name they recognize? How can they find out more about this author? Are the author's credentials listed? What kinds of credentials would make this author more trustworthy? More questionable?

Explore links. All scholarly publications have bibliographies or resource sections that show us where the authors got their information. We can check the facts. We can find verification for the claims made. When an online resource includes a digital bibliography in the form of links to other sites, students have a great tool for evaluating the credibility of the information on that page. These links can also help students expand their research.

Consider "understandability." When reviewing a possible source, students must ask themselves, *Do I understand the words I'm reading?* You might think that students would shy away from material that they don't understand, but reports filled with misinformation and misused technical terms have convinced me this is not always the case. For example, a student who goes to Wikipedia with the question "What causes obesity?" will find a whole section labeled "Causes." So he copies what he finds there, including that obesity is caused by "an obesogenic environment" and that "childhood obesity likely is the result of the interaction of natural selection favouring those with more parsimonious energy metabolism and today's consumerist society" (Wikipedia, 2014a). Say what now? Students need to be sure they understand what they're reading before they write or cut-and-paste it into their notes.

If they don't understand the language in the articles they find, one option is to tell them to find another source. But what if the source is authoritative and contains valuable information? Then you might advise students to look up terms they don't understand and translate them into words they do. We can find out that an *obesogenic environment* is an environment that promotes weight gain. And what kind of environment does that? One where inactivity is encouraged and high-calorie foods are readily available. Yes, some articles will be so far beyond students' comprehension that Option 1 is the best choice. But if that isn't the case, a little more work can lead them to a better understanding of the topic. This is what research is all about.

Action Item: "Form"-alized Searching. Create a form that your students can use to evaluate online resources in terms of the categories we've discussed (appearance, purpose, ownership, authority, and understandability), and make it a standard first step in your classroom's research protocol. You might set it up like a report card ("Give every site you consider an *A, B, C, D,* or *F* in each category"), or you might favor your own rating systems (5 = Awesome Resource for This Project, 1 = No Way This Works). The key is for students to evaluate every potential source in all categories and give it a Thumbs Up or Thumbs Down. I recommend using a small form, something that fits on a standard notecard or that can be reproduced in multiples and sliced so that each student has a handful to use (see Figure 3.2). Consider including comment spaces where students can indicate how the site earned its grade or rating.

FIGURE 2: **A Simple Form for Source Evaluation**

Criteria	Source 1	Source 2	Source 3
Appearance	B	C	A
Purpose	B	C	B
Ownership	C	D	A
Authority	A	F	A
Understandability	C	B	B
Verdict	⇨	⇩	⇧

Wikipedia Evaluation

Although many would disagree with me, I don't think Wikipedia is something to be afraid of or to ban from the classroom. Still, the main objection to Wikipedia is easy to understand: those who are generating and editing Wikipedia entries may have no expertise in the subject. Wikipedia is quite clear about this:

"Lack of authority"

Wikipedia acknowledges that it should not be used as a primary source for research. [7] Librarian Philip Bradley stated in an October 2004 interview with *The Guardian* that "the main problem is the lack of authority. With printed publications, the publishers have to ensure that their data is reliable, as their livelihood depends on it. But with something like this, all that goes out the window." [8] Robert McHenry similarly noted that readers of Wikipedia cannot know who has written the article they are reading—it may or may not have been written by an expert.[9]" (Wikipedia, 2014b)

Personally, I lean toward allowing a Wikipedia citation in student research papers as long as it is corroborated with other scholarly sources. The key to every Wikipedia article can be found at the bottom of the page—the "References" and "External links" sections. A quality article will be well backed up with these bibliographic resources, and you should encourage students to click on these links and do a little additional digging to verify the accuracy of the sourcing. If students don't find references or can't back them up, Wikipedia articles deserve the same skepticism as other material that is not sourced or attributed to an authoritative author.

Action Item: Wiki-ing. Pull up a Wikipedia article with an Edit tab on the upper right. (In my workshops, I use the article "Baseball Rules." Even though the rules of baseball have been unchanged for some time, clicking on the View history tab reveals that the article has been altered many times recently.) Now, model for students just how easy it is to edit an article. Click the Edit tab. Select some text and delete it. Add some text. Change the font to italics. (Don't submit these edits, though; you'd be making a mess for someone else to clean up.)

At the end of your demonstration, you want two points to be clear: (1) researchers must treat Wikipedia with suspicion because anyone—including non-experts and vandals—can edit pages and introduce erroneous information; and (2) researchers must not edit Wikipedia pages while they are researching.

Finally, scroll down to the bottom of an article to show students "References" and "External links," and ask them to use the information provided there to assess the value of the article and determine how it might further their research. The more comprehensive and credible a wiki article's documentation, the more useful it can be.

Using Online Resources

At this point in the research process, all students will have quality information that they can understand and use, right? Not so fast. It's extremely likely that some will have gathered information that still needs to be properly cited and attributed to its source, some will have gathered information that they actually don't understand at all, and some will have gathered information without considering how it fits into their task or objective. As a teacher, you still have work to do, and it involves guiding students' use of the information they've found.

Steering Clear of Cut and Paste

A student in the 2nd grade gives an oral report about the country assigned to her: "My country is Brazil. The economy is agriculture. A famous person is Peel [*sic*]. The main geography is Amazon." She reproduced information from the Google Safe Search for Kids results (mostly) correctly, but does she have any idea what these words mean?

Student research reports filled with language that their writers do not understand is a common occurrence in the age of Internet research. The power of "cut and paste" makes information all too easy to capture, and students can generate reports without doing a whole lot of critical thinking about the information they're presenting. When you don't learn from research, what's the point of it? As your students begin their online research, stress that they must be sure they understand the information they're capturing and plan to use. And never set up a final project that can be completed without understanding.

Action Item: In Other Words 101. With younger students, consider a "Say it Two Ways" report in which each fact presented must also be explained: "The main geography is Amazon." *And?* "The Amazon is a big jungle in Brazil." Another approach for elementary students is to create and distribute a two-column form. Students can put the exact quotes they find (cut and pasted, if the form is electronic) in Column 1 and then put a paraphrase of the quote in Column 2. For older students, consider unorthodox presentation formats. Instead of assigning individual short speeches on a topic, try an "Ask the Expert" panel in which three students conduct a three- to five-minute interview of the "expert" who did the research, asking follow-up questions about anything they didn't understand and probing for clarity.

Avoiding Plagiarism

Like most students, I wrote a lot of reports in school, and I didn't always invest them with a lot of critical or original thought. If the encyclopedia entry read

> Inspired by Eeyore's success in the restaurant business, Winnie decided to pursue a career as a chef . . .

. . . in my report, I might have written this: *Winnie decided to pursue a career as a chef because he was inspired by Eeyore's success in the restaurant business.*

It never occurred to me that there might be something wrong with this. If I were going to school today, the ability to cut-and-paste from online sources would have made my work that much easier: Grab the entire sentence, highlight the second clause, Ctrl X, move the cursor to the beginning of the sentence, and Ctrl V.

The kids I taught wrote a lot for me, and I knew their writing well. When one of my students turned in a paper featuring a couple of lines clearly written by someone else, I returned the paper with those sentences highlighted and a question: "Plagiarism?" He pointed out that it was only two sentences. *Is* that plagiarism? How about when a student submits a PowerPoint that includes some images copied from Bing Images. Is *that* OK? What about if the student goes on to include those images in a video that is posted on YouTube. Does that change anything?

Plagiarism is using someone else's work and trying to pass it off as your work. This definition contains the idea that there must be a deliberate attempt to hide the source and make readers or listeners believe the ideas you're expressing are original to you. For better or worse, the Internet has made it extremely easy for students to find ideas. Our challenge is help them see why they should never let someone else's work stand in for their own. Stress to students that plagiarism can have very serious consequences. At many universities, it will get them expelled. Let students know that you will use plagiarism detectors if you notice suspicious writing. There are several free tools that can be very helpful here, including Plagiarism Detector (http://plagiarismdetector.net) and Plagiarism Checker (www.plagiarismchecker.com). Both of these tools essentially do a Google search of words you entered—one on the exact phrase and another that shows you all words highlighted individually in various online resources. You could also do this searching yourself, pasting the suspect phrase, in quotation marks, into the search box and going back to add the prefix *allintext:* (e.g., *allintext: "childhood obesity is the most important problem facing kids today"*). Other websites will check papers for a fee per paper or per subscription. Turnitin.com (http://turnitin.com) is perhaps the best known of those.

Action Item: Plagiarism 101. Share the provided definition of plagiarism with students. Send older students to Plagiarism.org (www.plagiarism.org) before they begin to write, or use the free materials provided there for some class lessons. Some of the examples of plagiarism will surprise them. (It's possible to plagiarize your own work!) Stress that there is no acceptable amount of borrowing without attribution. Yep, taking only two sentences out of an entire book *is* plagiarism.

Citation Issues

Maybe I am naïve, but I tend to think students are not consciously trying to pass off others' work as their own as much as they are failing to give the creator of the work appropriate credit or even understanding that credit is required. I believe that most of the "plagiarism" we see in student work is due more to a lack of understanding than to an intent to deceive.

The first response to suspected plagiarism, then, ought to be a conversation rather than punishment, and that conversation needs to focus on the importance of giving credit where credit is due. We can also provide specific instruction focused on what needs to be cited and when. The answer is not as black and white as we might wish. Here are a couple of tests to pass on to your students.

The Common Knowledge test. The key question to ask is *Does everyone know this?*

Teachers frequently assign book reports (Palmer, 2014).

I did make this point in my 2014 book, but does that statement need to be followed with a citation? No. Everyone knows that teachers assign book reports. I didn't say anything unique and original. When something is common knowledge, it does not need to be cited. Of course, the Common Knowledge test really introduces a sliding scale. How common does the knowledge need to be? Let's look at some examples.

- *Many children today are overweight.* Almost all of us have heard that. It's common knowledge, and no source is required.

- *One third of kids and teens are overweight or obese, triple the number from 1963.* There are specific dates and statistics here that are not common knowledge and definitely came from someone's research or research analysis. The source is required: American Heart Association, 2014.
- *Being overweight may lead to heart problems.* That is common knowledge for family physicians, probably common knowledge for most adults, and probably NOT common knowledge for elementary students. If my doctor told me this, I wouldn't ask for his source. If my 4th grade student told me this in a report, I would ask, "How do you know this?"

What is common knowledge, then, depends on the writer's age, level of education, training, occupation, and more.

The Original Idea test. This test's question is *Did I think of this, or did someone else think of it?* It wasn't my insight that Winnie-the-Pooh wanted to be a chef because of Eeyore; I got that idea from someone else. Likewise, my student didn't come up with those two sentences on his own. If the ideas a writer puts on the page are not original to the writer, they need a citation.

Action Item: Citation Central. Get students in the habit of writing down all of their sources. The minute they decide that a source is good (perhaps guided by the assessment tool you gave them), they should write citation information on the back of the notecard. As appropriate for your grade level, include some or all of these: author, date published or posted, title of the article, web address, and date retrieved. Stress that it is better to have information that may not be needed than to find out someday that information is needed and hasn't been recorded.

How to cite. Have you ever gotten something like this in a paper? *According to www.IGotInfoFromHere.com/crazy-stuff$/morecrazystuff&symbols/&/@html, many people don't eat well.* Yes, of course you have. The good news is that as you work to make students aware that the information on websites doesn't just exist—that it was created by someone— they will understand that they should cite the creator, not the address. This kind of "citation" should begin to disappear.

There are official ways to cite favored by the Associated Press (AP style), the University of Chicago Press (Chicago style), and so on, but I don't think we want to bury students in concern over specific citation formats, especially when they are young. As a teacher, I want to know where the information came from, and I want to be able to find the source to verify that information, if I need to. If I can do it with the information the student provided in the bibliography, I am OK with not following Chicago style. Come up with a citation form that works for your students, or follow any prevailing style that might be favored in your school or department.

Action Item: In Other Words 201. Provide specific instruction on the skills of paraphrasing, summarizing, and citation, and model them for your students by taking a text and showing the various ways they could use its information in a report. Let's use an excerpt from an article in *Scientific American* for an illustration:

> In three decades child and adolescent obesity has tripled in the U.S., and estimates from 2010 classify more than a third of children and teens as overweight or obese. Obesity puts these kids at higher risk for type 2 diabetes, cardiovascular disease, sleep apnea, and bone or joint problems. The variables responsible are thought to range from too little exercise to too many soft drinks. (Haelle, 2013, para. 2)

This is plagiarism—unacceptable:

> Surprisingly to me, over one third of children and teens are overweight or obese. Why in just 30 years, child and adolescent obesity has tripled in America. This can cause problems. Heart disease, diabetes, sleep apnea, and bone and joint problems can happen. Too many soft drinks and not enough exercise may be responsible.

This is a paraphrase with citation—yes!

> Tara Haelle talked about the problem in an article in Scientific American. She noted that over a third of children and teens are overweight or obese, a percentage that is triple what it was in 1983. She mentioned that type 2 diabetes, heart disease, sleep problems, and bone/joint problems may be risks of being overweight. She suggested that not enough

activity and too much pop may be causes of obesity (Haelle, 2013).

Finally, here's a short summary with citation—also good!

One writer pointed out that over a third of kids are overweight, which may lead to heart, sleep, joint, and/or diabetes problems. Inactivity and sugary drinks may be part of the problem (Haelle, 2013).

Copyright and Fair Use

A student holds up a poster. Pasted on it are some pictures cut out from a magazine and some notecards with writing. Bubble letters at the top say "Childhood Obesity." That is what visual aids used to be. Appropriately, new standards are pushing students toward multimedia presentations—including podcasts and videos that are being posted on wiki pages, web pages, and YouTube. As student work continues to cross the line into published work and public performance, it's more important than ever to teach the basic rules of copyright and fair use.

If it's posted on the Internet, it is OK to use, right? It's already out there, so isn't it fair game? What if I give the author credit—just add a citation? Short answers: no, no, and yes, you have to do that, but it may not be enough.

It is not fair to put students into the position of wrongdoing because they didn't know better. It is not fair to surprise them after the podcast has been created with the news that they cannot use the music or various images because these works are copyrighted. It's up to us to teach them these things *before* the presentation is designed. When assigning projects that involve media, be sure to share information on the following topics in a form that your students can understand.

Public domain. Some material is available to all of us for all purposes. Usually, these are older works where copyrights may have expired or never existed.

Copyright. Text, images, audio, and video are protected by copyright law, and in the United States, formal copyrights are issued by the Library of Congress to those who submit materials. In a practical sense, copyrights protect content creators, keeping people from using their work without permission. In the eyes of the law, copyright is automatic. Without even having to apply, products produced are protected for authors, musicians, photographers, and filmmakers. This does not mean that others are forbidden from incorporating these products into their own otherwise original work, but to do so, they must follow explicit terms of use, issued by the copyright holder, and often pay a fee. It is always an option to ask copyright holders for permission to use their work. Because the process can take a long time and be expensive, it's best to guide students in other directions.

Fair use. As with the Common Knowledge test, there is a sliding scale for what constitutes fair use. The U.S. Copyright Office lists four factors to consider:

1. What is the purpose of the use? For nonprofit educational use? For commercial gain?

2. What is the nature of the work being used? Something factual? Something highly creative?
3. How much of the work is being used? A small percent of the whole? A substantial amount?
4. Will the use possibly affect the market of the original work? Will the creator lose money? (2012, para. 3)

Educational uses are more likely to be allowed. Creative works are more likely to be "protected"—excluded from fair use. Small extracts from works are more likely to be OK. If what you want to do with the copyrighted material will cut into the creator's ability to make money from the work, it is probably not fair use.

So: Using 30 seconds of a hit song in a student podcast played for the class? Fine. Using the entire song as a soundtrack for a student video posted online? No. Putting a picture from the *Denver Post* in your class presentation? OK. Using that picture as the cover for a story you are offering through your website? No. A graph downloaded from a *Scientific American* article added to the PowerPoint you will use for a class talk? That's OK, too.

Creative Commons. Many content creators are more generous than copyright law suggests. They are happy to share their creations, but they do put restrictions on how that work can be used. The online archive Creative Commons (http://creativecommons.org) was established to let content creators choose ways to share work: e.g., anyone can use this work for any purpose as long as attribution is given, this work be used as long as it is not for commercial gain, and so on. At the site, students will find links to music and images that can be freely used. It is an excellent classroom resource.

Action Item: Hunting Licenses. Search for an image using Google images. When the results appear, click on Search Tools, which will reveal a drop-down menu that allows you to restrict the results by image size, color, time (e.g., past 24 hours, last week, exact date), and, the part we want to focus upon, *usage rights,* which can take you to images that have been labeled for fair use or have a Creative Commons license. Lead older students in an exploration of free media sites like FreeDigitalPhotos.net (www.freedigitalphotos. net) and FreePlayMusic.com (www.freeplaymusic.com). At FreeDigitalPhotos.net, search and browse various topics, review the standard license, and look at the specific terms of use indicated for specific images. At FreePlayMusic.com, show students how they can use search words to find pages marked to match various uses. Students can enter search words (*happy, afraid, energetic*) to find music that matches the mood they are trying to create in a presentation or video.

Developing Lifelong Skills

At the beginning of this book, I stated that I wanted to provide a practical approach for preparing students to conduct truly effective online research. I hope you feel like I've done my job. I think it is also worth pointing out that the skills and understanding students gain when we share this information with them goes far beyond our class research projects.

Nearly every day of their lives, students encounter material online, and they need to be able to evaluate and make sense of all of it. We want them to learn about the topics they're researching and master the research process, but we also want to further their development as critical thinkers and web-savvy consumers of information. When we prepare them to conduct quality online research, we prepare them for so much more.

To give your feedback on this publication and be entered into a drawing for a free ASCD Arias e-book, please visit **www.ascd.org/ariasfeedback**

ASCD | arias™

ENCORE

A CHECKLIST FOR TEACHING ONLINE RESEARCH SKILLS

I wrote about Naperville North High School in *Teaching the Core Skills of Listening & Speaking* and mentioned that all students doing Internet research fill out a website evaluation checklist before they begin taking notes. I think all teachers should fill out a checklist like the one that follows before they send students online.

Some of the items in this list may not apply to your grade level. For instance, elementary teachers should put N/A in front of "My students have looked for a scholarly journal." The more items you can check off on the list, the more likely it is that your students will have the tools they need to be successful online researchers.

Before Students Go Online
- ☐ My students know that the Internet is a network of linked computers, not a single, infallible source of information.
- ☐ My students know that the web is a collection of resources specially formatted to be searchable.
- ☐ My students know that a browser is a software program designed to access the web.
- ☐ My students have generated a list of specific, targeted questions to focus their searching.
- ☐ My students know how to use AND, OR, NOT (&, /, −).

☐ My students know how to use quotation marks to search for phrases.

☐ My students know about "site:", "filetype:", "related:", and other search shortcuts.

Going Online to Seek Answers

☐ My students know that a search engine is a program that scours the web looking for resources containing the key words being searched.

☐ My students know that a variety of search engines exist.

☐ I have told my students that these search engines may be particularly useful for them:

_____

_____

_____

☐ My students know that our school library has subscribed to a number of library databases.

☐ I have told my students that these databases will be especially useful:

_____

_____

_____

☐ My students know that the local public library has a variety of library databases.

☐ I have recommended these databases:

_____

_____

_____

☐ My students have looked for a scholarly journal related to their topic.

Evaluating Information

☐ My students know the difference between .com, .org, and .edu.

☐ I have given my students a form to use for evaluating websites.

☐ My students know not to begin taking notes without first examining the website.

☐ My students know how to find "About Us" information, how to truncate URLs, and how to find a site owner.

☐ My students have been told to avoid writing down information they don't understand.

☐ My students know what Wikipedia is and why they should be cautious when using it.

Using the Information

☐ My students know not to use words or information in their final project that they don't understand.

☐ My students can define plagiarism.

☐ My students understand how to paraphrase and how to cite.

☐ My students have a simple form for filling out citation information.

☐ My students know about public domain, copyright, fair use, and Creative Commons.

References

American Heart Association. (2014, August). *What is childhood obesity?* Retrieved from http://www.heart.org/HEARTORG/GettingHealthy/ HealthierKids/ChildhoodObesity/What-is-childhood-obesity_ UCM_304347_Article.jsp

eBizMBA. (2014, August). Top 15 most popular search engines. Retrieved from http://www.ebizmba.com/articles/search-engines

Google. (2014). Privacy and terms. Retrieved from http://www.google. com/policies/terms/

Haelle, T. (2013, April 9). Consumption junction: Childhood obesity determined largely by environmental factors, not genes or sloth. *Scientific American.* Retrieved from http://www.scientificamerican.com/article/ childhood-obesity-determined-largely-by-environmental-factors/

Kolata, G. (2013, April 7). Scientific articles accepted. (Personal checks, too). *New York Times,* p. A1.

MedlinePlus. (2013). About MedlinePlus. Retrieved from http://www. nlm.nih.gov/medlineplus/aboutmedlineplus.html

Palmer, E. (2014). *Teaching the core skills of listening & speaking.* Alexandria, VA: ASCD.

Pew Research Center. (2012, November 1). *How teens do research in the digital world.* Washington, DC: Pew Research Center's Internet & American Life Project.

United States Copyright Office. (2012). Fair use. Retrieved from http:// www.copyright.gov/fls/fl102.html

Wikipedia. (2014a). Childhood obesity. Retrieved from http:// en.wikipedia.org/wiki/Childhood_obesity

Wikipedia. (2014b). *Criticism of Wikipedia.* Retrieved from http:// en.wikipedia.org/wiki/Criticism_of_Wikipedia

Wikipedia. (2014c). Welcome to Wikipedia. Retrieved from http:// en.wikipedia.org/wiki/Main_Page

Related Resources

At the time of publication, the following ASCD resources were available (ASCD stock numbers appear in parentheses). For up-to-date information about ASCD resources, go to www.ascd.org. You can search the complete archives of *Educational Leadership* at http://www.ascd.org/el.

ASCD EDge®
Exchange ideas and connect with other educators interested in various topics, including Project-Based Inquiry Learning, on the social networking site ASCD EDge at http://edge.ascd.org.

Print Products
Authentic Learning in the Digital Age: Engaging Students Through Inquiry by Larissa Pahomov (#115009)
Teaching with Tablets: How Do I Integrate Tablets with Effective Instruction? by Nancy Frey, Douglas Fisher, and Alex Gonzalez (#SF113074)
Using Technology with Classroom Instruction That Works by Harold Pitler, Elizabeth R. Hubbell, and Matt Kuhn (#112012)

ASCD PD Online® Courses
Project-Based Learning: An Answer to the Common Core Challenge (#PD13OC008)
Technology in Schools: A Balanced Perspective, 2nd edition (#PD11OC109)
These and other online courses are available at www.ascd.org/pdonline.

DVD
The Innovators: Project-Based Learning and the 21st Century (#613043)

For more information: send e-mail to member@ascd.org; call 1-800-933-2723 or 703-578-9600, press 2; send a fax to 703-575-5400; or write to Information Services, ASCD, 1703 N. Beauregard St., Alexandria, VA 22311-1714 USA.

About the Author

Erik Palmer is an educational consultant from Denver, Colorado, and the author of *Well Spoken: Teaching Speaking to All Students; Digitally Speaking: How to Improve Student Presentations with Technology;* and *Teaching the Core Skills of Listening & Speaking.* He is a program consultant for Houghton Mifflin Harcourt's English language arts programs, Collections and Journeys. Erik presents frequently at state and national conferences, and he has given keynotes and led in-service trainings in school districts across the United States and Mexico. He can be reached through his websites: www.erikpalmer.net and www.pvlegs.com, his website specifically devoted to listening and speaking.